THE DARKEST DAYS

Sean Michael LaValley

THE DARKEST DAYS

SEAN MICHAEL LAVALLEY

ISBN 978-0-6151-4547-1

Four walls high

With open sky

A Paris Trip

My suicide

Bleeding wrists

Yield wings that fly

To all I love

Goodnight. Goodbye.

My sky has grown cold

And I'm cast to the shadows

Beaten and raped of my mind

So I lie on the land

My mouth full of sand

And I smile

For I didn't die

Blind

Fresh Dreams

Invade the day

Her ginger glow

Is sticky on me

Like candy rainbows

That bleed carefree

In the night

Between Our Dreams

There are small spaces

Where often I fall

Upon reflections of

Your warming grace

My mind halos around you

In dream, in life, and in wonder

Many dreams, in fact, are pure

Instances of wanting, hope

Sleep trances devouring lonesome hours

My one true wish come love

You, a true come dream

It's been a while since we have spoken

The flowers I promised to dry

Have long since wilted and died

I miss you

I fucking miss you

Fish bowl, intoxicating consumption

Sushi, on fire

My mouth and body burn for you

And you laugh

In the days to come

I predict new sadness

Raining on white lilies

Blue madness embracing

The world imperfectly filthy

Greenest of demons in envious passion

Driven by women who

Are solemn and ashen

There's not enough time

In all of the world

For all of our dreams to come true

So, if I had the chance

To choose only one

The one dream I'd choose would be you

I've searched the sky

Through and through

And found a star

Just for you

I have it here

Here with me

And it's glowing

Very beautifully

Inter laden violet grace

Wears violently upon my face

My song, it plays its melody

As rain melts gently onto me

Scared to dream, the night is young

And I'm afraid of everyone

My scriptures done

My song is sung

Goddess Grove

Down on Goddess Grove

Where the demons used to play

I found a love that rid me of

All my shades of gray

Canto Triple Six

Spoiled

The flesh has ceased being fresh.

Elegant necrosis

Body still and silent

Pavement sticky from

Children's screams

Warm smiles surpass the marrow

The man with the red coat is missing

I know where he keeps his sunshine

In a locked box beneath his bed

With the gun in which he healed his head

Voices ran through walls of blue

Into the heads of those who knew

I burned my mouth swallowing night

I had stardust upon the lips I kissed you with

Your mouth now sparkles like the sky

Close your eyes

The whole world

Goes away

Beauty reigns

From your

Bright light

Down on me

With soft delight

Gentle wanting

Pure and white

Enter we

The velvet night

Tonight,

The planet was absorbed

With black cosmic energy

Eclipsed visions

Of full purple moons

Dance over our enormous oceans

Sweet desire, strong lust for her love

Deep into a red wine autumn

We suffer through

Our stained glass nightmares

Dream with me, love

Dream of me, love

Of only me, love

Let's run to our forever, together

Steal the sun

Taste the earth

Witness birth

Together, forever, as one

If I told you

I would dance for days

On rainbows and shadows

On tombs and on graves

Would you take my hand

Hold me tight

Let me die in your arms tonight

Perplexed visions

Incumbent resurrection

Beauty filled

Sweetly sainted

Alone now

Here we are

Angels dancing

All around

Us tonight

The night is

Burning black

With twisted

Smokey stars

Sky on fire

We rejoice

Consummate

Our new love

By starlit

Silent seas

You and me

Together free

I love you

Winter Day in May

Rainy Days

And cobblestone walkways

Dancing through the tears

As heaven melts us all away

Melts us all away

On this winter day in May

Raging beauty in a world of betrayal
How can I see the light
Encompassed by fear in the depth of our hearts
Haunted by angels we see in the night
Candles flicker
Their flames burn our eyes
When seeing your truth
My dream slowly dies
Living this birth
A haunting nightmare
I search for the warmth
That never was there
Holding me back
With a soft spoken lie
Fingers caress
As I choose to die…
…Long live that
Which brings me sorrow
In hope that I
Will be dead by tomorrow
Condemned by the silent
Wish for such love
I despise the sweet angel
Who was sent from above
Searching for innocence
I've heard your last lie
I give up to you
And then wonder why
I didn't die

Stranger than life

Attraction

Amazing beauty

Who wouldn't

Fall in love

With emeralds

Enter tonight with me

The cool midnight

Burns bright

I kissed her mouth

And death wept

The night is amazing

Dressed in black

Jeweled with silver stars

And perfumed with

The sweet scent

Of loneliness

Sing sonnets to the sky

We welcome it's

Sullen silence

Planets beneath

We walk on stars

That line the streets

And set sail on our ship

Made of stone

The sun drips wet with caustic flames

I watch it paint the sky insane

Eternal height

Hysterical madness

Over vast tides of

Everlasting tragedy

I seek to dream you

Sweetly with open

Eyes, unconscious mind

The world is ours

Embrace with me the

Beauty of its countries,

The texture of its culture

And the integrity of

Its will to change

And Forever Reigns With Brilliant Madness

Silk soft the tongues

Of warm weeping angels

Deep be the blood

For we've fucked god away

Bodies unfolding

Like lone desert flowers

And loud are the wails

That bury their day

Minds on high

Dream wild of sunshine

Their silence speaks

In foreign prose

Gently numb

And timidly humid

Together, one

Morbidity grows

Eyes awake in early dawn

Ghosts await to free

Their spawn

Souls rejoice

The girl is gone

And above all else

Your god was wrong

Explosion

I ejaculate flames

That give rise to sensual gods

Warm snakes insane

Burn through your sinful garden

Elevate we, in euphoria

We dance in subliminal lunacy

For your divine ALMIGHTY

Rented the hooker's womb

And planted his Jesus seed

Born to die and spread

His lie, the masses eat his flesh

With no question as to why

Where the evening angels gather

Is where I want to be

Off in the Parisian distant

The tower of light explodes

Falling in love through the midnight

On the river on which we rode

Melting as one through the midnight

On the river on which we rode

Elevate in descending rhyme

Her remarkable magic

Glows in brilliant black

She-demon of magnificent magnitude

Melting mountains with cruelty

I and the world are at your feet

My rose it grows

For you to see

It's thorns like horns

Press light we bleed

The face of stone

Fixed and free

Melts slowly as

You're beating me

...and the solar system fails magnificently

Mercury falls a million miles below the sun

Creating a warm galaxy for the moon

To absorb and reflect eternity

My Graceful Suicide

Bathing deeply in

The forgotten sea

I recall my

Favorite memory

A time when heaven

Was torn asunder

And I inhaled three

Years of thunder

Times that I had

Witnessed sadness

And blessed the gods

With gentle madness

Times I laughed

And times I cried

A time I lived

And chose to die

Along the shore there lie ancient angels

Wearing tired hearts around their cement souls

The curiosity of night is companioned with

Immaculate silence that swells in the lungs of all

dreamers

Who am I to stone this sky

Arch angel of crystal can you hear me

I am dying, dear one

The earth has stopped spinning

And my world has stopped trying

I'm living beneath a demon who's dreaming

Of large black twisting flames…

That dance and curse and call our names

Tired, slowing, and morbidly growing

I kiss the soft sky to sleep

I weep and I weep in my misery deep

And die as the wind stops blowing

My Masterpiece

Blood and skull on canvas

My brush is chrome

And loaded

The sky cascades

The mountains bleed

The sun unfolds

For you to see

A day bathed in

A rare beauty

That lulls us to

Eternity

I Glow For You

At the cool lake calm

Sit and stare

Angels dancing everywhere

Fall to dream

Of visions fair

As the wind blows heaven

Through your hair

Awake, the day

Seems more than new

And the sun has turned

From gold to blue

You ask it why

It glows this hue

And the sun replies

"I glow for you"

My baby, she waits

She screams loud the sea

My baby, it's late

Come quick, rescue me

I thought I could sail

The world for its sky

But I lost my true treasure

On my next breath, I die

As I cry, love, goodbye

I'm lost in the tide

I'm bleeding, I'm screaming

And I'm not brave...

I lied

She walks on pride through my mind

She breathes frozen sunshine up my spine

She dances wicked flames right by my side

I alive

I can no longer perceive

My transient reflection in

Your ephemeral rainbow

I can, however

Witness my pulse

Radiating around

Your brilliant halo

A marvelous feeling

A marvelous feeling

In deed

Beaten like a dreadful drum

Halo burning blue and numb

Legs are broken, can't outrun

The demon and her glowing gun

Recite for me

My eulogy

With all intent

I'll be set free

Explaining death

And dark destiny

And what is left

Of this eternity

...And in the loveliness

Of perpetual abstraction

I fall witness to a

Continuity of true love

Harmonious, articulately penetrating

And blissfully everlasting

I slaughtered the demons

That stormed through my mind

I ripped out their tongues

And fucked them all blind

I buried them all

In dark shallow holes

And exhumed them all later

To set free their souls

Explain to me the mystic's motion

Breathe me in envy and wish me away

I've beaten my dreams to sleep

And I have witnessed the sky's blue burning

I've kissed gods to life

And brought them to death with a whisper

In the rain I scream

Insanely to the sky

I dance the world alive

Arms on fire, I summon all stars

Of the union, respectfully, none

Compare to thee

Lost obscene

In eyes of green

I beckon my

Goddess to breathe

She then takes me in flight

Where her wings, warm

Ignite, and she bathes me in

The moons eerie light

My dreams

They bleed in harmony

With your sleep

Free forming

Monsters of beauty

And decadence

I glory in this miracle

We have created

Enter night

We sail soft in the sea

In search of an ancient

Egyptian sunrise

The gods kiss our ship

Through the sky

We awake

The pharaoh is on fire

And the sun bleeds apparitions

Of your face

Strangulate

Come see what I see

Turn blue with me

Swallowing stones that breathe

An empty breeze and these

Winter seas wash over me

And freeze

Believe

Be my halo

Shining bright

Upon my face

For the rest of life

Hallucinating Rain

I

Bright she burns with fever sweet
I can taste the sky upon her feet
Melting mourn, hallucinating rain
Through her eyes I fall insane
Inhale deep her poison breath
And set free my demons when I sense death

II

Run child wild, run away free
Escape this dreary life with me
We can climb through the sky
In search of our stone
And fall to a world
Where we could dream all alone

Here the pharaoh sings

Cobble stone streets

Lined with ancient death

We follow the silence

To inspiration

I weep at the site of stone

In the element of evening

How sweet you're desired

The monster alone

Masturbates by the fire

A vision he senses

His mind summons spasm

His body alive

At the height of orgasm

Indecent and awkward

I'm spinning webs of words

Around worlds of empty wombs

She speaks of lands green and freezing

Warm is the sun as the snow feels her face

Engaging in life like new desert flowers

Witnessing wisdom as they invade with grace

Lone ship of stone docked silent by seaside

The night beckons silence from ocean and air

Enter the warmth, a world we call magic

She speaks of this world, but I know, I was there

The Darkest Days

I
She spins me in
Uncertain circles
And lends me balance
With her kiss

II
Adorned with grace
My dreams, they beam
In silver space
What seems to be
A voiceless face
So beautifully
Staring silently at me

III
In the dawn of time
New creatures are born
Strange and pretty
Young beings of silk
Bare witness to the
Strange encounter of life
We excel in solitude and despair
Lonely we, in the tide of eve
Stomachs full on egotistical sickness
And mealworms twist and secure our guts
Alone we encounter new night
We sleep in sound trances
And beg for awkward amnesty
From non-existent gods
We, imbeciles

IV

Cool collective conscience
Soft and free sentiment
Nurture and nature
Eloquent equestrian
Pleasure breeds in your
False face

V

She-goddess burning
In warm velvet spirals
In love with thy goddess of night
Alone by the tide, two
It's warm deep inside you
As we bathe in the new
Neon moonlight

VI

Blackest of orgasms
Send warm snakes through your womb
And together tonight, love
This sea is our tomb

www.ingramcontent.com/pod-product-compliance
Lightning Source LLC
LaVergne TN
LVHW011413080426
835511LV00005B/516